What Do We Know About
RAINFORESTS?

PETER BEDRICK BOOKS

NEW YORK

First American Edition published in 1992 by
Peter Bedrick Books
2112 Broadway
New York, NY 10023

Copyright © 1991 by Simon & Schuster
Young Books

Published by agreement with Simon & Schuster Young
Books, Hemel Hempstead, England

Author *Dr. Brian Knapp*
Art Director *Duncan McCrae*
Illustrator *Mark Franklin*
Designed and produced by
EARTHSCAPE EDITIONS,
86 Peppard Road, Sonning Common,
Reading, Berkshire, RG4 9RP, UK
Printed and bound *in Hong Kong*

Library of Congress Cataloguing-in-Publication Data

Knapp, Brian J.
    What do we know about Rainforests? (Caring for environme
Brian Knapp. — 1st American ed.
    Includes index.
    Summary: A geographic survey of the earth's
rainforests, their climate and ecological importance.
    ISBN 0-87226-358-4
    1. Rain forests--Juvenile literature. 2. Rain forest
ecology--Juvenile literature. 3. Rain forest
conservation--Juvenile literature. 4. Man --
Influence on nature--Juvenile literature.
[1. Rain forests. 2. Rain forest ecology. 3. Rain
forest conservation. 4. Ecology.] I. Title. II. Title:
Rain forests. III. Series
QH541.5.R27K63   1992
574.5'2642'0913--dc20   92-5187
                                                    CIP
                                                    AC

Picture credits

t=top b=bottom l=left r=right

All photographs from the earthscape Editions
photographic library except the following: Bruce
Coleman 22t, Andrew Mendes 14t, 38t; The
Huthchison Library 29b, 35b, 36, 37;
Kate Simpson 23; ZEFA Front cover, 24t, 30t

CONTENTS

1: WHAT ARE THE RAINFORESTS?

Rainforests receive enough energy to support a multitude of creatures. *Here plants grow in great profusion even in the dim light of the forest floor.*

Rainforests – the forests that naturally clothe the land near to the Equator – are among the world's greatest treasures. They often reach the news because their future is of great concern, and they are frequently the subject of films. Yet despite this publicity, rainforests are some of the least well understood regions of the world.

People often call rainforests 'jungles'. This is a word that is easy to say, yet it is a name properly used only for one kind of rainforest: the kind where people have destroyed the original trees and where new saplings are springing up and competing for the light. A jungle

In undisturbed rainforests *each tree jostles its neighbors in a never-ending fight to get enough sunlight.*

is a forest recovering after a disaster such as logging, a place where there is little room for movement and relatively little variety in the wildlife. It is a long way from the more open rainforests that are undisturbed.

Rainforests are our most ancient natural lands. The effects of the world's great droughts or the ravages brought by the **Ice Ages** have all passed the rainforests by. Here the wildlife does not battle against the weather as it does in other parts of the world. The climate has remained steady, with plentiful warmth, sunshine and moisture, for millions of years.

The wet rainforests are ideal for creatures such as tree frogs.

In the ancient rainforests nature has been able to produce a bewildering variety of species. This is one reason why, to the casual observer, the forest appears to be alive with resources. There are high trees of massive girth, good for timber, and for nuts or fruit. There is soil, far deeper than in any other part of the world, and there are animals of all shapes and sizes. This truly appears to be a bountiful land, and one that can supply all the needs of people who want to live there.

Yet in this land appearances are cruelly deceptive. It is a mistake to think of giant trees as a never-ending supply of timber; it is a mistake to think of the deep soils as suitable for crops; and it is a mistake to imagine that rainforest animals can successfully be replaced by herds of domestic animals. It is through such mistaken impressions that the rainforests have been subject to such savage attack. Too late have people learned that rainforests are fragile lands that must be treated more carefully than almost any other place on earth.

How people can survive in the rainforest, how they can benefit by its great resources, and how it can be preserved for future generations to enjoy, depends on understanding how the rainforest has evolved. This is described in the first part of this book. The second part of the book describes how people have tried to live in the rainforest and why they have often been defeated by it. The final part is about how we can look after the rainforest, especially in areas which are under great pressure from people.

Rainforests are no longer as widespread as in the past because the land has been used by people for other purposes. Rice fields are one of the better ways to use rainforest land: rice is the highest yielding of all cereal plants.

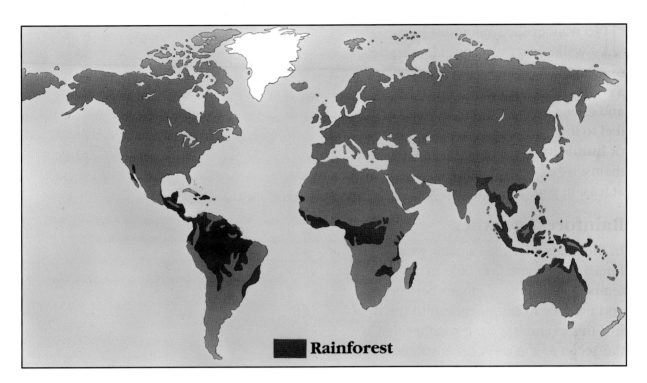

The natural extent of the world's tropical rainforests *is shown on this map. Many of these areas have now been cleared for farming or commercial tree-growing.*

In a natural rainforest many people live very isolated lives.
The main arteries of communication are often the rivers and the rainforest has mainly been exploited through its waterways. The highest concentrations of people are also found beside the rivers, although increasing numbers of roads are changing this traditional distribution and giving people access to previously remote places.

2: THE ENVIRONMENT

To walk inside a rainforest is like walking in the tropical hot-house of a botanical garden: here you will find a constant temperature of about 86°F and enough moisture to give a sticky feel to the air. Much of the moisture, or **humidity**, is produced by the plants themselves, because the rainforest makes, at least in part, its own climate.

Rainforest weather

In the lands near the Equator weather forecasters would find little to do. The temperature hardly changes between day and night or from one month to the next. It is this evenness of the weather that is the secret to the rainforest's success.

The tropical humid weather and the forests are closely linked. *This picture shows the forest 'steaming' after a rainstorm. There is a constant exchange of moisture between the air and the trees. If trees are cut down in large numbers this exchange cannot take place; there will be less moisture in the air and less rain will fall. In turn this could make conditions too dry for the remaining plants.*

The tropics provide the heat engine that powers the whole global circulation *of the atmosphere. Intense heating by the sun causes air to rise near the Equator. This zone of rising air is marked as 'low pressure' on weather maps. This is the place where thunderstorms are produced.*

From this region air spreads out at high levels and sinks to the north and south where it creates the great deserts. Rainforests only exist below the region of rising air where rainfall is reliable.

Each day the sun rises quickly in the sky and heats the ground intensely. The warmed air then rises, drawing moisture from the surface and carrying it high into the sky where it cools and forms the water droplets that make clouds.

By lunchtime the sky is filled with clouds and by mid-afternoon it is pouring with torrential rain. In some parts of the world rainstorms occur very regularly each day for months on end. People can almost set their watches by them. In other places there is a little more variety, with a few months being less wet and more sunny than the others. But the key to a rainforest is that there should be enough rain so that the plants do not dry out, the pattern of rain ensuring a continuing supply of water for all the plants that grow.

Soil

When people walk through a rainforest their feet are cushioned by a layer of fallen leaves. They could hardly guess that below them lies one of the most unusual soils on earth, a place where rocks are constantly under attack from the warm, moist conditions.

All soil is formed by the destruction (or weathering) of rock. As the rainwater flows through the soil, it acts like a diluted acid, slowly breaking down the rock and carrying away the soluble products of decay. In the rainforest this process has been going on unchecked for millions of years. In many places the soil is now many yards thick, tens of times thicker than it would be in other parts of the world.

The thick, old soil is mainly made of clay. It is a sticky material that will not easily wash away. But over the years rainwater has washed the **nutrients** away, leaving the soil quite infertile. In many soils, rotting has reached such a depth that there are no more rocks near the surface to be weathered and release supplies of nutrients for the plants. This situation has forced plants to adapt to survive. They are the world's best scavengers, capturing nutrients from the rain and dead plants to make up for what they cannot get from the soil.

This soil has been exposed in a road cutting.
The great thickness of weathering is exploited by using bulldozers to make cuttings. You can see the bulldozer scrape marks on the soil face. Few plant roots have penetrated the soil: there is nothing there for them to use.

The land

In the hot humid soils beneath rainforests, the rocks are turned into clays and few stones ever find their way to river beds. Without this natural 'sandpaper' to help to scour the channels, rivers in rainforest lands have little erosive power and they mainly cut insignificant valleys. The landscape is only carved into deep valleys and hills near to mountains. As a result, the vast majority of the land is dominated by flat plains.

The only rocks that are not attacked by tropical weathering are called **quartzites**. They are made of a material that has the same kind of chemistry as glass. This material is almost immune to chemical weathering, and cannot readily be attacked by rivers because they do not have the stones to wear it away. As a result, quartzite rocks are responsible for some spectacular waterfalls.

The Kiteur Falls on the Potaro river in Guyana occur where an unusually tough bond of rock resists the normal chemical attack of rainforest acids.

A surprise underfoot! This boulder has been taken from deep inside a cutting made by a bulldozer. It looks sound enough and most people would not risk dropping it near their bare feet. But when this boulder is dropped it proves to be so rotten that it simply smashes into tiny clay fragments.

Water streams down in front of the open door of this hut in the tropical rainforest. It is mid-afternoon, but the sky has turned dark and become obscured by the torrential downpour.

Living with the weather

The hot, humid conditions of the tropical rainforests are difficult for people. It is impossible to work hard for long periods without becoming very fatigued and risking collapse through **heat stroke**. The high humidity makes matters worse because the normal cooling effects of sweating are ineffective.

People in the tropical rainforests have traditionally worn little clothing, exposing as much skin as possible to any cooling breeze that might be available. Houses are designed to let air circulate as freely as possible. Shelters are used to keep dry in the rain, and possibly as protection against animals during the night. All buildings feature large openings (windows), and walls that have an air gap between the top and the roof.

Because there is a high risk of rainwater pouring over the floor of a house built on the ground, many people construct their homes on stilts. The space below the floor doubles up as a shelter for domestic animals at night.

3: FOREST WILDERNESS

You might think that plants and animals living in the rainforest find life much easier than in other areas of the world. After all there are no gales to blow down trees and no frosts to kill buds and shoots. There are not even any droughts which may force animals to migrate to other areas in search of food.

But this warm, rainy and very stable world is not as tranquil and easy as it seems. Indeed, survival in the rainforest is as difficult for its inhabitants as any other place on earth.

Finding a niche

The tropical rainforest is a naturally occurring collection of plants and animals that live in balance with the soils and climate. This **ecosystem** survives because every species is constantly battling for space in which to thrive and reproduce.

There is enough energy and moisture for a wide variety of species to find a **habitat** or niche that will suit their requirements. But a home is often suitable for more than one kind of inhabitant and there is often great competition between species.

The most prodigious plants are the rainforest trees. Reaching up to well over 150 feet from the ground, these trees capture much of the sun's energy in their dense canopy. Unlike trees in cooler regions, tropical trees can get their energy from a relatively small area of leaf. So they do not grow side branches, but instead race high into the air where they then spread out in the form of an umbrella.

Straight, tall trees leave lots of space for other kinds of species to grow among the giant trunks. Smaller trees and saplings, waiting their turn to be larger trees, occupy this open space. They cannot expect to get as much energy and their growth is slower. They often have large leaves to help to expose themselves to as much light as possible.

Even the dim light that filters through the tree canopy provides enough energy for a profusion of plants to grow. Here the stream banks are dominated by ferns, some of which grow to over 16 feet high.

Silent hosts

The giant trees provide much more than a dimly lit space between their trunks. They also provide a home and a structure on which plants can lean. High in the branches are plants that have no roots, but simply cling to their host tree using it as a convenient support. Bromeliads are among the most common of this type of plant, called an **epiphyte**. Their rosettes of leaves are specially shaped to funnel the rain down to the center, and here nutrients are extracted directly from the water. It is a signal that plants do not necessarily need soil to get the food they need to survive, as we shall see later on.

Many plants are more demanding of their hosts; they are using them as way of surviving. Figs, of which there are innumerable species in the rainforest, wind up the trunks of large trees, using them to climb high into the forest canopy. At the same time they strangle the tree on which they are climbing, and often sink sucking rootlets into its bark to gain extra nutrients.

Figs provide many of the **lianas** of the forest, dangling branches that look like gnarled ropes from some monster cobweb.

In a rare break in a rainforest mountainside, a stream forges a narrow path. Notice how close the tree canopy has grown, and how the undergrowth plants near to the stream have grown up to take advantage of the extra light that reaches the ground

Bromeliads live in the moist space below the main canopy. Their rosette shape helps to focus rainwater to the center, where it is stored until the plant can take out the nutrients. It is easy to see this work because bromeliads are common household plants.

One means of attracting pollinating insects near the ground is to provide large, bright flowers. Notice the broad leaves that are used to gather as much energy as possible.

How trees ward off their enemies

Most rainforest trees are evergreens. There are no harsh seasons to force them to shed their leaves and so leaves grow and are renewed throughout the year. But this continuous green canopy can easily become delicious food for a myriad of animals that live in the forests. So to combat them the tress have many survival strategies.

Some trees spread out near their base to give broad 'fins' which are called buttresses. They look as though they grow like this to support the massive tall trunks, but in fact they probably spread out to give all the roots the best possible chance of finding nutrients in the poor soil. The thin trunk growing between the buttresses is part of a fig tree.

One important means of survival is to attract large animals to their fruits. Many trees have luscious fruits that animals such as monkeys will eat whole. Then, as the monkeys move from tree to tree, they will scatter the indigestible fruit pits with their droppings. So not only has the animal benefited from the food, but the tree has gained from having its seeds dispersed to new growing sites.

Spreading seeds

All plants need to disperse their seeds because there are many hungry animals waiting to devour every leaf in sight. Fortunately for the trees, many insects – the most dangerous creatures for plant survival – have very specific eating habits. Each species often gets its food from the leaves of only one or two species.

If there were many trees of the same species growing side by side then a plague of insects might easily devour the trees one after another. But because each species of tree has scattered its seeds so well, plants are also widely scattered, making it much harder for insects to find each new plant to devour.

Trees do not just survive by chance, however. Many have tough bark and leaves to make them less easy to digest, while many others develop poisons in their leaves which make them dangerous for animals and insects to eat.

Self-sufficient trees

Many rainforest trees are so huge that it might seem inconceivable that they could survive in anything other than the most fertile of soils. And so it certainly seemed to many people who tried to cultivate the forest. But nothing is quite what it seems in a rainforest. For example, the giant trees often appear to prop themselves up with widely splayed roots called **buttresses**. Yet these buttresses are really not capable of holding the tree upright. What they are actually doing is making it possible for the roots to spread further in their search for food.

Trees in a rainforest have to be the most efficient plants of all, because the soil is not very fertile. The deeply weathered soils are, in fact, so old that all the rocks from which they are made weathered long ago. Millions of years of rainfall have washed away most of the nutrients and the soils are now **acid** and impoverished. Indeed, no trees could readily grow in such soils from scratch. But fortunately rainforest trees have an amazing network of roots that manage to scavenge all the nutrients. And, although they are the giants of the forest, their survival is helped by some of the most minute organisms of forest life.

An example of a tree being used as a prop by a climbing species. Like an ivy, this plant has small roots all along its stem which it uses to hold fast to the bark of its host.

Fungi hold the key

As the roots spread out in a network through the soil, they do not go downwards through the soil in search of minerals and water; there are, after all, no minerals and water is plentifully available. Instead, they grow just under the surface, sending up multitudes of tiny rootlets to the layer of rotting leaves scattered on the soil. Here a strange relationship occurs, whereby the root tips make use of microscopic fungi to digest the leaves and then transfer the nutrients to the roots.

This elegantly patterned butterfly is just one of thousands of tropical rainforest species. Each butterfly is a specialist, flying at its own special height and feeding from selected plants. It is the enormous variety of flowering plants that makes this possible.

In this way the trees manage to recapture the nutrients that were lost when they lost their leaves. And any tiny surplus that escapes can be made good as the roots soak up the minerals from each fresh rainstorm.

So it turns out that the trees are amazingly self-sufficient, that the soils are infertile, and that the forest survives only because there is an incredibly tight network of species all helping each other.

The roots of tropical rainforest trees stay near the surface where they can use the nutrients released by the decaying leaves. Here you can see the white rootlets literally on the soil surface.

Macaws are sociable, brightly colored birds that are high canopy species, living and eating in the trees.

Their sociable habits have many advantages for survival. They operate a 'Neighbourhood Watch' scheme. With a combined total of several hundred eyes in a troop, they can readily spot a predator and send out a raucous squawking warning.

The many layers in this rainforest give an idea of the diversity of habitats in which creatures live.
The most dangerous place, and the one with least food, is the exposed forest floor, which is the reason why most animals are tree-dwellers.

Forest animals

Although the forest contains a wealth of animals, most people visiting a rainforest would see hardly any of them. Perhaps most conspicuous would be ants and beetles, some of gigantic proportions like the Goliath beetle shown on this page. Most of these are the decomposers of the rainforest ecosystem. They are clearing up the dead bodies and lost fruit and nuts that fall from the canopy above.

A Goliath beetle, shown here in life size, is one of the largest insects in the world, with a wingspan of up to 1 foot. One of the immense variety of insects that exists in a rainforest, each finding a special niche in which to survive, the Goliath beetle flies in the tree canopy where it eats fruit from the trees. Its larvae are wood-boring.

Monkeys are typical of the mammals that live in the middle branches of the canopy. They eat fruits in the trees as they move within their large territories and scatter the pits in their droppings.

A surprisingly large number of rainforest creatures live in the high branches. From monkeys and bats to macaws and butterflies, they are drawn to the high branches by the food growing on the trees. Because the trees have few lower branches there is relatively little to eat near the forest floor. By contrast there is nectar and fruit and fresh new leaves in abundance within the canopy. Equally important, it is also a relatively safe place, for the forest floor is home to carnivores like the leopard and tiger.

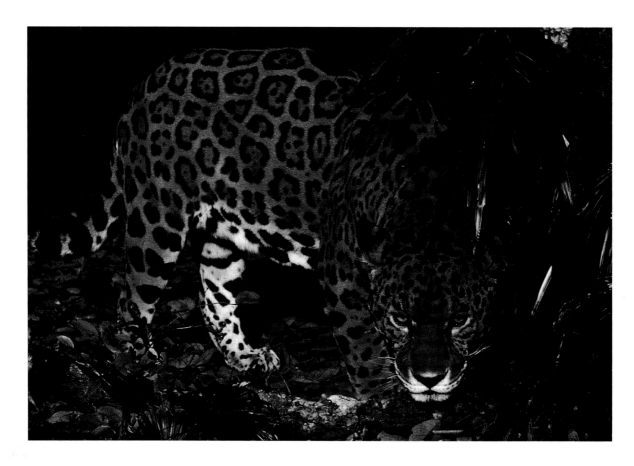

Jaguars are among the top carnivores in the *rainforest ecosystem. Their food consists of many of the forest mammals and, because of this, they have territories which may range over tens of square miles.*

Many of the forest animals are very selective feeders. Their food may come from just one or two species of trees. And because the trees are so widely scattered, many animals have to forage far and wide to get enough to eat. This means that if we are to care for the forest animals, we must appreciate that they need large spaces to find their food. Small thickets left to grow here and there amidst cleared land are not sufficient.

How a rainforest is renewed

Many rainforest trees attain a great age, but eventually each tree will die and crash to the ground. When this happens it may well cause other trees to fall as well, thereby opening up a space in the forest canopy.

wThe light which beams down to the ground in the resultant clearing triggers an enormous amount of life into rapid activity. For many years saplings have been staying almost **dormant**, waiting for such an opportunity. Now, with the extra energy from the direct rays of the sun, they spurt into growth, shooting upwards as fast as they can.

It does not take very many months for the once-open ground beneath a closed canopy to be transformed into a dense and often almost impenetrable jungle. Every species is making the most use of the sunlight while it lasts. But within a few years the strongest and most vigorous of the saplings will have won the race for the light, and they will send out an umbrella-shaped fan of branches whose leaves will start to create shade below.

The losers in the race often stop growing as the light is shaded out, and many others die away. The successful trees begin to close over the canopy and the ground is once more poorly lit and humid. The change, or succession, has taken its full course and the mature forest is re-established.

The conditions for renewal

The renewal of a forest takes place all the time. Animals are constantly eating fruits and then carrying the seeds away to be deposited on the forest floor. Beneath all mature trees there are saplings and seeds waiting to take over when the time comes. And they have to be quick, because the soil is so infertile that the nutrients released by the dead tree as it rots must be taken up by the new trees as they build their stems and leaves.

The race for survival can only be successfully fought in small clearings where the right conditions exist for new trees to spring up when their ancestors die. New rainforests colonize bare open ground very slowly because the conditions are not humid enough for the seeds and saplings to survive. Unlike weeds and grasses that can thrive in dry, open and sun-baked soil and which will rush in to colonize an area that has been cleared, a rainforest will retreat much more easily than it will advance.

The competition for space shows very clearly where a river cuts through rainforest in the Congo, West Africa. Each tall trunk thrusts up to get part of the sunlight that reaches the canopy.

4: USING THE TREES

This boy from the South American rainforest *has found a vantage point from which he can shoot at his quarry.*
Tribespeople can still find a good livelihood in the undisturbed areas of forest as hunter-gatherers.

The rainforest is truly a treasure trove for mankind. Rainforests contain the largest mass of tree material in the world. The trees are often hardwood and make fine building materials and furniture timber. The huge variety of species also means there is a tree for every purpose. The trees are therefore a great temptation to those who would make money from the forest.

What the trees can offer

Rainforest trees can provide people with all the necessities of a simple life. They can provide building materials that give homes and furniture; they provide fuelwood for cooking and heating; their nuts and berries provide

Some of the more common fruits, nuts, herbs and spices found in supermarkets have their origins in the tropical rainforest. There are many other wild plants that could be cultivated.

Forest crop	Tree type	Origin
Banana	understory tree	SE Asia
Brazil nuts	canopy tree	Brazil
Avocado	understory tree	Guatemala
Passion fruit	climber	Brazil
Pineapple	bromeliad family	Paraguay
Lemon	understory tree	Burma
Lime	understory tree	Malaysia
Tapioca	swamp forest	Malaysia
Robusta coffee	understory tree	West Africa
Cocoa	understory tree	West Africa
Vanilla	orchid (climber)	SE Asia
Oil palm	understory tree	West Africa
Cloves	understory tree	New Guinea

food; and their sap provides materials that can be used for everything from sugar to cooking oil and glue. The trees also provide homes to a wide range of species that can be hunted for food.

The trees can also offer something that is less obvious. Because there are so many species, and because rainforests have existed for such enormous lengths of time, they now form the most valuable source of **genetic** material on earth. Scientists are only now beginning to understand how to make use of their properties to help provide medicines, and to feed the future world.

The hunter-gatherers

The people who have lived in the forest the longest are also the most knowledgeable about its ways. These peoples, often living as small groups or tribes within the main forests of Africa, South America and Southeast Asia, have learnt how trees can be used as food, as shelter, and even as medicine.

Some of these people do not cultivate the land at all. They are hunter-gatherers, relying on their ability to kill animals with bows and arrows or blowpipes, and their knowledge of where to find edible roots and seeds.

A selection of the fruits and nuts that can be readily obtained in our supermarkets and which come from rainforest trees.
You may be surprised at the variety.

Because there is no dry or cold season, the forests provide food all year round and they do not need to store or preserve foods.

The number of hunter-gatherers depends on the resources the forests can provide. If there are too many people relying on one area for their food, they will go hungry and may starve. For this reason hunter-gatherer tribes have always lived in small, widely spaced groups, each giving themselves enough territory for their survival.

Hunter-gatherer people are so dependent on the forest that they have had to learn how to live with it, how to make sure they do not over-harvest or destroy it. Much of this knowledge is passed on from generation to generation as rituals and religious ceremonies, thus ensuring that everyone is sensitive to their use of the forest.

Passion fruit

Banana

Brazil nuts

Lime

Harvesters

Tribes can harvest for their own use, but they can also harvest a surplus for sale. They can harvest not just nuts, like the Brazil nut, and fruits, like the banana, but also the sap of many trees, like the rubber tree. They can also crush the nuts of trees, like the palm, to make oil. Some trees even have a fragrant bark which can be cut and smoked to provide a pleasant aroma – a kind of incense.

Harvesting can be difficult, however, because each species of tree is widely scattered for its own protection. And while this is important for natural forest survival, it can be an inconvenience to the harvester. Not surprisingly, therefore, people have long sought to gather the most useful trees together to make the harvest more economical.

Just as in cooler regions there are orchards for collections of apple trees or orange groves for oranges, so in the tropical rainforests, many areas have been cut down and replaced with one or two species of tree. Each area of replanting is called a plantation.

The pictures above show the way the bark of the rubber tree can be scored to tap the sap. The white latex liquid is collected in a cup and then cured over a fire. Rubber collecting is done by smallholders and companies.

The picture to the right shows the way a rainforest has been replaced by **stands** of rubber trees on a hillslope. Rubber trees are shallow-rooted and do not protect the soil well. Widespread rubber plantations have been blamed for the increased flooding and loss of life that has recently occurred in countries such as Thailand.

Plantations are the oldest type of forest farming. The idea is to use the trees in their natural surroundings where they will grow well, but in patterns that will allow people to harvest the trees efficiently. Plantations are often managed by individual families (when the plantation makes up part of a smallholding) or they are organized into huge holdings managed by a company. These groupings of plantations are called estates, and were the way that former colonial countries organized the forests of their colonies. Because it is an effective system of farming, estates are still commonplace today – some government-controlled, others run by private companies.

New for old

At first sight, the replacement of a rainforest with plantations of useful trees may seem to bring nothing but benefit. There is, after all, still a forest, and the tree cover remains intact. However, this is to miss the point about rainforest survival. There is good reason for the wide spacing of trees of similar species in a forest: it is to prevent the spread of disease or the ravages of pests. A plantation can be wiped out by an uncontrolled pest in a way that would never be possible in a natural forest.

Some improvements to protecting the soil can be made by growing crops on the ground beneath the trees. These are pineapples growing beneath rubber trees.

This is an oil palm plantation. The rainforest has been replaced with trees which have been regularly spaced. Notice the way the ground is kept clear. This is very different from a natural forest. With trees planted together in this fashion they are very vulnerable to attacks by pests, and strong pesticides have to be used regularly.

Some of the more useful trees for people do not naturally make up the main tree canopy, but are weaker trees that naturally live in the understory. Rubber trees are a common example. Rubber trees do not make a close canopy of leaves to keep out the effects of the torrential rainstorms and so they do not protect the soil as well as a natural forest. They do not have roots that can hold fast in a wet soil and they will readily fall over when planted in rows on a slope. So although people have gained the rubber resource, they have lost many of the valuable aspects of the forest.

Loggers

The loggers see the rainforest merely as a resource to be mined. They take away and they do not replace. Indeed even if they wanted to replace they could not: the rainforest is too complex an environment for simple replanting, and in any case people do not yet know how to raise many species in nurseries.

Loggers only cut down the trees that other people want. In general there is the largest demand for the biggest and tallest trees, and especially for those with the hardest wood. But these are the very trees that have taken longest to grow. A hardwood is hard because it grows slowly; it will not be replaced readily.

You can get some idea of the impact of logging by trying to picture a table with pencils standing end up all over it. Now imagine trying to take a pencil from the center of the table out sideways without disturbing any of the others. Clearly it is impossible. In the past elephants were used to pull the logs from the forests. Elephants are extraordinarily careful and soft-footed animals and their impact on the forest was as small as it could be. Today, however, machines are used. They are faster, but much more destructive for the environment because their caterpillar wheels rip open the soil surface as they move along.

An area of forest that has been clear-cut.
The soil is left exposed and will erode with every storm. This is the most destructive form of logging.

The traditional way of taking logs out of a forest *was to tie them to an elephant by a chain. The elephant would then pull the logs to the collecting point and then lift them into piles with its trunk. Logging by elephant was slow and this meant that there was a limit to the speed at which a forest could be exploited. Because elephants did not need roads, the forest remained relatively inaccessible and undisturbed.*

The new way of taking logs *out of a forest relies on bulldozers and trucks. Not only do the machines destroy the soil surface, but they also need more room than elephants to move about. Access roads are also vital if the logs are to be taken quickly to markets.*

5: FROM FOREST TO FARM

It takes more than teamwork to clear an area of rainforest successfully. *These women and children are preparing a 'garden' in the ashes of the forest, but they are unable to move the larger branches and stumps.*

Two things have caused great concern for rainforest lands. The first has been a rapid growth of population, meaning more mouths to feed and a consequent need for more farmland. The second has been a change in the farmers. Now the majority are those who have been driven by pressures to the forests from elsewhere. They are not natives to the forest and they do not understand how quickly they can cause disaster.

Moving on

The forest can stand a certain amount of exploitation, but no more. If the land is cleared and used for farming for a short

Shifting cultivation can take place round a fixed village site . Here the village clearing also shows the remains of stubborn stumps that the people cannot remove. The bare ground on the right is waterlogged and provides a new breeding place for parasites that does not exist in the native forest. At the same time the clearing has no protection against rain and water simply runs over the surface.

The blackened branch of a tree shows that this land has been recently burned for farmland. The rice (the grass-like plants in this picture) is growing well, but so are the 'weeds'. When the land is abandoned the weeds will take over and rebuild the forest.

while and then abandoned, in time the trees will grow back in place. Forest peoples have cut and burned small areas – often known as 'gardens' – for countless generations. Because their tools are simple they cannot cut and remove the tree trunks. They simply set fire to a patch of forest and plant in among the burned and fallen branches and trunks.

For a few years the ashes from the forest will provide the nutrients that domesticated plants need. Maize, 'dry' rice (that does not need flooded land) and many vegetables will grow well enough under these conditions. But as soon as this temporary supply is exhausted the yields will fall and the

people will have to abandon the worn-out land and clear another area.

This practice is called shifting cultivation. Using shifting cultivation, a small tribe will need a large area to live on. But as populations grow and more people try to get food from the land they will be forced to replant before the land has recovered. Then, not only do they get poor harvests, but the forest never gets a chance to recover.

Paddy farming

The swampy lands near to rivers may seem best avoided, but it is where the oldest form of farming started – rice growing.

'Wet' rice, or paddy rice, is a curious cereal because, unlike all the other major cereals of the world, it thrives on water. Indeed, it cannot live unless the land is flooded while it is growing.

For thousands of years people have cultivated rice in fields that have been reclaimed from riverside swamp. And over the years people have learned how to manage this system well.

Each field is surrounded by a wall that keeps the water in, and each is connected by a system of feeder canals which admits fresh water from rivers. In addition, an equally vital system of drains lets stale water out of the fields before it stagnates.

Paddy farming uses the land intensively. As a result there is little room for forest trees, except the productive ones such as bananas or palms.

Even smallholders can often hire machinery to help them with the more tiring tasks of paddy farming. Here a special plow turns over the muddy soil after the fields have been drained. The white 'sheets' hanging on the line in the background are mats of raw rubber that have been collected from nearby trees.

This type of farming – called paddy farming – has been successful for so long because it uses the land in a sensible way. Rice has a higher yield than any other cereal. This means that large numbers of people can be sustained on relatively small areas.

Paddy farming traditionally used the land near to rivers because it is rich in nutrients drained from the rest of the rainforest.

Traditional wet rice cultivation is not a severe burden on the land, but uses nutrients that have been naturally fed to the fields. Rice farmers have many generations of experience to guide them in how to manage their land. And unlike the people who make gardens in the forest, the paddy farmers never need to move to new sites because they receive a constant supply of nutrients from the rivers.

As soon as the fields have been plowed they are flooded and rice seedlings are planted. For most people this is a back-breaking job.

As the rice grows this smallholder hoes between the lines of rice to prevent weeds from growing. Notice the wall separating the fields and how one section of it has been broken down to allow water to flow from one field to the other.

Newcomers to farming

There are many newcomers to the forest who are unskilled in the techniques needed to deal with it and through their ignorance they have caused widespread devastation.

Each continent has its own story to tell. In Indonesia they may have migrated from the densely populated paddy lands of Java to the almost unpopulated rainforest of Sulawesi. In Brazil they may have come from the drought-ridden northeast to the rainforests of the states of Amazonas and Rondonia.

But wherever they have come from, it is almost certain that the stories they have heard will have been false. There is a saying that a little knowledge is a dangerous thing. Nowhere is this more apt than in the fragile rainforests. The knowledge that the newcomers have is often no more than hearsay. They choose to believe that the land is dark, rich and fertile. It is not.

To run a farm needs more than back-breaking toil. It needs seed, proper techniques and a market to which to sell. The peasants are often too poor to have any of these. Many arrive, work the land without success and then leave. But there are always thousands more to follow, willing to chance their luck, not knowing how heavily the odds are stacked against their success. They, and the cattle ranchers who destroy forests and plant grass, are the farmers who threaten the rainforest the most.

The problem that many peasants face *is that they have no knowledge of the soil or the effects of rainfall on bare soil. They are too poor to afford fertilizers and so must adopt the tribal ways such as burning the forest to clear it and release the nutrients stored in the trees; yet they do not have the tribal experience. Governments give peasants fixed areas of land which they are forced to overuse, whereas the tribespeople move from area to area as the soil becomes exhausted.*

This is typical of land that has been cultivated without knowledge. The long thin lines of crops can do little to prevent soil erosion. Before long this sloping field will be stricken with deep gullies that will make the land unworkable.

While peasants tend their small plots, some large companies have bought vast areas of rainforest to turn into cattle ranches, seeing the cheap land as a way of making money.

These companies should have the resources to know better. Instead they show surprising ignorance of the capabilities of the land. Despite the use of the latest machines and doses of fertilizers, grasses have grown poorly, cattle have caught diseases, and no-one has made any money. Large tracts have been abandoned and the rains have eroded the soils. Both people and the environment have lost.

6: OUTSIDERS

Outsiders are people who do not naturally live and work in the rainforests. They are people who do not value the land except as a resource to be mined or used in some other way.

For many poor peasants their dream is to find an outcrop of gold ore that will make them wealthy and allow their families to lead a better life. For the large corporation and government department the goal is to make use of the wide range of minerals that lie buried. Gold may be one of these, but as much wealth can be made from iron, aluminium, tin and copper – all plentiful under the rainforest soils.

The search for gold

People have always sought to find gold and make their fortunes. The people who now search in the South American rainforests, for example, have the same objectives as the people who made their fortunes in California or in Alaska's Klondike during the nineteenth century.

There are probably hundreds of thousands of people mining in the rainforests. Even so, their impact might not be important but for two things. First, their arrival opens up the forest. Roads are built to bring services to them

and soon towns develop. With towns come more permanent settlers and the end to the natural forest. Second, and just as important, the techniques the miners use are primitive and harmful to the environment. In particular the miners use mercury to extract gold from the rock. A small digging can pollute and poison a stream for tens of miles downstream.

Untapped wealth

Peasants like the Brazilian 'galimperos' do much damage, but their efforts are puny compared with the damage that can be done by large commercial organizations using open-cast mining methods.

Open-cast happens like this. First a large area – often many hundreds of square miles – is cleared by burning and bulldozer. Then the soil is pushed to one side. Below the soil the rotted rock contains perhaps iron, aluminium or copper. Even a rock with just one or two percent of copper is a rich find, so just imagine how much rock has to be bulldozed and put through smelting machines to yield a million tons of metal. And the companies are after many millions of tons a year in order to pay back the cost of the equipment and make a profit.

The people working in this mine are called **galimperos**. *They are the peasant miners of Brazil. This is the most famous, and most productive mine in Brazil, called Serra Pelada. Fortunes have been made here, though few will be made in the future because the hole is too deep and the sides are constantly collapsing. The fact that, despite the dangers, people keep working here is an example of how desperately poor these people are. Given this degree of poverty, these people cannot be expected to show any real degree of care for their environment.*

Miners disturb vast amounts of soil and **rock**, *then they wash it to reveal the gold. The washings return to the rivers where they make the water muddy and unsuitable for many kinds of wildlife. In the mining process many dangerous heavy metals are released into the water. As a result mercury poisoning is now commonplace amongst the people who drink river water near to mines. The metals also build up in the fish and other river creatures. This not only kills the animals but helps to poison people when the animals are eaten.*

Smelting

Smelting means heating rock until the metal runs free and can be tapped off. To make the heat either coal, oil, gas or charcoal have to be used. In the rainforests, coal, oil and gas supplies are not easy to get. But all around lie forests which can be cut down and made into charcoal.

Smelting means that the miners not only clear the forest for the ore, but far worse, they clear enormous areas of extra land to fuel the hungry furnaces. In fact the forests are destroyed so quickly by this means that there would be little chance of keeping pace by replanting even if large scale efforts were made – and they have not. As a result the search for minerals represents one of the forest's more serious dangers.

Power to the people

One reason whypeople in developing countries are poor is because many of them have to spend so much of their money paying for imported oil. Governments in such countries see any large river as a way

Most rainforests occur on gently sloping land. When dams are built to supply hydro-electric power the water stored behind them often reaches for thousands of square miles.
When trees are even partially drowned they soon die.

of generating hydro-electricity. But this means that many rainforests are in danger from flooding. No-one will use the timber, the trees will simply be drowned.

Countries have set about dam building projects with gusto. The only problem is that many countries now have more electricity than they know what to do

This is a small area of the land that was used for open-cast tin mining and then abandoned.

All of the species that have been planted around the patio by this swimming pool grow naturally in the rainforest. Here they have been selected for their decorative properties.

This part of the Malaysian coast has been changed to make room for a hotel complex. Some mature palms have been left, and others have been planted. Grass now grows between the trees. This gives the tourists a comfortable place to sit and admire the sun as it shimmers over the sea.

with. The forests have often been destroyed for no purpose. Building these large schemes is the wrong way to help the majority of the people.

Making a vacation paradise

The climate that gives the warmth and rain to make a tropical rainforest can also provide the ideal place for a vacation. Many areas whose natural vegetation is rainforest are described in the vacation brochures as 'Tropical Paradise'.

But to make the coastal rainforest into an ideal tourist resort requires much effort on the part of the hotel trade. First the forest has to be cleared to make room for hotels, golf courses, roads and airports. Most rainforest trees look very straggly when they are exposed by forest clearance. Many are replaced by palms transported from inland plantations. Then, when all this has been done, and the land manicured and made to look nice, the tourists will arrive, but the rainforest will have gone.

7: IS THERE A FUTURE?

We can only care for our environments if we understand the way they work, *and* appreciate the reasons they are threatened. For example, we cannot just try to save the trees in a rainforest without worrying about the insects because every living thing is part of a balanced cycle, or ecosystem. Soil, plants and animals are all dependent on each other.

We also have to understand that the way a rainforest works is unique. It cannot be managed in the way we might manage, say, a temperate woodland. A rainforest survives because its species are widely scattered. In turn this means that, if we want to preserve the rainforest, we cannot simply preserve scattered clumps wherever it is convenient because then many of the species will be missing, and others will have too little room to scatter their seeds. Clearly the only way to preserve the natural forest is in very large tracts of undisturbed land. Even a road and cleared verges can be too much disturbance if it makes the land more accessible to people and drives wildlife away.

Matching wealth to care

People have to have a reason to care. The hunter-gatherers of the rainforests must care because their way of life – their survival – depends on the rainforest. People in the developed world with ample to eat can afford to care because they do not depend on the rainforest for their survival. In between lie a range of people each with their differing motives.

Hardwoods can be carved into beautiful furniture. *Rainforests will continue to be destroyed unless plantations of hardwoods are established.*

You might not recognize this piece of a rainforest *because it has been turned into a bowl. Beautiful though the bowl might be, if there is too much exploitation of the forest the only place the rainforest will survive in the future will be in people's houses!*

Many people simply want to make a better life for themselves. They would argue that they cannot afford to care because they are poor and the only way they can survive is through farming land. Governments sometimes say that it is their responsibility to improve the wealth of their people. This is why they allow logging, burning and mining.

Everyone has a right to a decent way of life. But the people who destroy the forest are not improving their lives in the long run, because in general their farms fail in the poor soil and the trees disappear, leaving them with no more forest to log. So it is important to make sure that fewer and fewer people need to destroy the forest. This is best done by making it easier for people to make their living in other ways.

No rainforest creatures will be safe while people throughout the world still pay high prices for the skins and furs of wild creatures.

Industry not only uses large areas of forest, but it is often a cause of pollution in the air and in rivers. Caring for the rainforest involves keeping tight controls on industry.

Giving the forest a wealth

Rainforests have wealth. At the moment it is the value of the hardwood trees for window frames and furniture. It is the soil for growing crops, and it is the rock for producing metal ore. But this could change. There are two ways to do this. One is to stop buying forest products. For example, if people did not buy tropical hardwoods then there would be no demand and fewer trees would be cut. But a better way is to give the forest more value when left alone than when used for logs and farms.

One way of caring for the rainforest and preserving logging jobs is to set aside plantations of hardwoods that can be replanted time after time. It therefore makes sense to buy hardwoods only from places with a replanting program.

Another way is to bring tourism to rainforests. Tourists spend considerable amounts of money. If a rainforest tourist industry develops in a way that makes people sensitive to the land, then it will be more profitable for local peoples to preserve the forest than to cut it down.

Beauty is in the eye of the beholder. *As more and more people begin to understand the wonders of a rainforest – often by seeing nature films on television – the more they will see the rainforest as a place of beauty and want to visit it. This picture shows the kind of landscape more people can enjoy.*

Seeing the dangers

People have to be made to see the danger to themselves of destroying the forests. This happened recently in Thailand where, in just twenty years, the country's forests were reduced from 80% of the land to under 20%.

As more and more trees were cut down and replaced with rubber trees or other crops, so the amount of water that could be stored in the soil became smaller. Finally, with each rainstorm there were devastating floods that killed many people. This helped the people to understand the damage they had caused, and the government was then able to put a ban on further logging with the consent of the people.

Simple facilities make all the difference to tourism. *It is not necessary to build huge hotels amidst the forest. This floating restaurant is a good example of simple, effective design that does little harm.*

Making National Parks

National Parks are used in many countries of the world to preserve areas as wilderness. They are only effective if they are big enough to allow the natural world to thrive.

It is easiest to set up National Parks before land comes under pressure. For example, many National Parks were set up in the western USA in the last century when there was relatively little pressure on the land. Now is also the time to set up National Parks in the naturally remote areas of the rainforests of the world. Venezuela has already set a lead in this, and some other countries have begun to follow. But a National Park need not be a place where all people are kept out, for the hunter-gatherer tribes will not damage the forests. People living in National Parks who depend on the forest for survival are the best guardians of the forest's future, for they will help stop people from logging and mining

Tin mining has left a terribly scarred landscape *. The remains of the rainforest will soon be destroyed as the cliff collapses. In trying to reclaim the tin mining land a golf course has been built to attract tourists. The ground has therefore been replanted to grass.*

illegally. This, too, has been the new Venezuelan policy.

In the end the way to preserve the forests is to take the pressure away. This means finding other jobs for the poorer people. It is not an easy task, yet until it is done the rainforests will continue to be under threat. Caring for the rainforest environment is a matter of understanding.

GLOSSARY

acid soil

a soil that has few plant nutrients in it and which is too poor for soil organisms to thrive. Most plants that live on acid soils have to be very efficient at recycling their own nutrients

buttresses

the name given to the fin-like structures that radiate out from the lower trunks of some rainforest trees. They are part of the root system and do little to hold the tree upright

dormant

a state where a plant or seed appears not to grow at all, but simply remains 'resting' and waiting for an opportunity to grow when conditions become right

ecosystem

a balanced arrangement of plants, animals, soil and climate. An ecosystem is a stable unit, with the decay of dead organisms providing the food for those that are growing

epiphyte

a plant that can grow without any roots, simply making use of the nutrients that wash in with the rainwater. Epiphytes grow especially well in places where rain is common, such as a tropical rainforest

habitat

the combination of environmental conditions that provide a suitable living environment for a species. An animal may find tree tops a good habitat; the habitat for a plant will include satisfactory soil and shade conditions

heat stroke

an illness brought on by overworking the heart in conditions of high humidity and temperature

humidity

the amount of water vapor in the air. Very humid conditions frequently occur in rainforests, allowing many creatures such as epiphytes to survive without any roots

Ice Age

a period when the world's ice sheets expanded greatly. As a result many areas lost their natural vegetation and it has only just recovered. The Ice Ages only made the tropical rainforest belt narrower, it did not change its character

lianas

thick stems and roots that seem to hang from trees in some types of rainforest. Many lianas are stems of climbers such as figs

nutrients

the essential foodstuffs that living things require to grow. Nutrients for plants are released when dead tissue is decomposed. Calcium, nitrogen and phosphorus are examples of common plant nutrients

quartzite

a rock made entirely from quartz. Quartz is commonly found on the beach as sand grains. It is a very stable mineral and will not usually weather

stand

the name given to a group of trees of the same species that occur together within a forest

INDEX